BLP

JEREMY LIN
Basketball Superstar

BY MATT DOEDEN

CAPSTONE PRESS
a capstone imprint

Sports Illustrated Kids Superstar Athletes is published by Capstone Press,
1710 Roe Crest Drive, North Mankato, Minnesota 56003.
www.capstonepub.com

Library of Congress Cataloging-in-Publication Data
Doeden, Matt.
  Jeremy Lin : basketball superstar / by Matt Doeden.
     p. cm.—(Sports Illustrated kids. Superstar athletes)
  Includes index.
  ISBN 978-1-62065-626-6 (library binding)
  ISBN 978-1-62065-627-3 (paperback)
  1. Lin, Jeremy, 1988——Juvenile literature. 2. Basketball players—United States—Biography—Juvenile literature.
I. Title.
  GV884.L586D64 2013
  796.323092—dc23   2012014232

Editorial Credits
Anthony Wacholtz, editor; Kozuko Collins, designer; Eric Gohl, media researcher;
     Eric Manske, production specialist

Photo Credits
AP Images/Elise Amendola, 12; Michael Dwyer, 15; Paul Sakuma, 17; Steve Yeater, 11
Getty Images/NBAE/Ron Turenne, 6
Landov LLC/Reuters, 9
Newscom/Icon SMI/Imago/Xinhua, 5
Sports Illustrated/Damian Strohmeyer, cover (right), 2–3, 19, 21, 23, 24;
John W. McDonough, 22 (top); Peter Read Miller, cover (left), 1, 22 (middle & bottom)

Design Elements
Shutterstock/chudo-yudo, designerpix, Fassver Anna, Fazakas Mihaly

Direct Quotations
Page 7: Associated Press. "Jeremy Lin Hits Game-Winning 3 as Knicks Top Raptors." ESPN.com. 14 Feb. 2012.
16 May 2012. http://espn.go.com/nba/recap/_/id/320214028/new-york-knicks-vs-toronto-raptors
Page 11: Dana O'Neil. "Immigrant Dream Plays Out Through Son." ESPN.com. 10 Dec. 2009. 16 May 2012.
http://sports.espn.go.com/ncb/columns/story?columnist=oneil_dana&id=4730385
Page 13: Jorge Castillo. "Harvard Graduate Jeremy Lin Blazes Unique Trail to Golden State Warriors."
Washington Post. 28 July 2010. 16 May 2012. www.washingtonpost.com/wp-dyn/content/article/2010/07/27/
AR2010072705802.html

Printed in the United States of America in North Mankato, Minnesota.

042012   006682CGF12

TABLE OF CONTENTS

CHAPTER 1

GAME-WINNING SHOT

Less than 10 seconds remained in a 2012 National Basketball Association (NBA) game. The New York Knicks and the Toronto Raptors were tied at 87. New York point guard Jeremy Lin had the ball.

Lin had become an overnight sensation in the NBA. In just a few weeks, he'd gone from an unknown player to a superstar. Could he continue his amazing run of success?

With five seconds to go, Lin made his move. He dribbled the ball to the 3-point line. The defender, Jose Calderon, backed up but stayed close to Lin. With less than a second on the clock, Lin pulled up and shot. Swish! Lin made a 3-pointer. The buzzer sounded and the Knicks won.

"I'm thankful that the coach and my teammates trust me with the ball at the end of the game." — Jeremy Lin

CHAPTER 2

ROAD TO THE NBA

Jeremy Shu-How Lin was born August 23, 1988, in Los Angeles, California. He was raised in Palo Alto, a city near San Francisco. He learned to love basketball from his father, Gie-Ming Lin. Gie-Ming took Jeremy and his two brothers to the gym to play. They watched NBA games to learn from the world's best players.

Jeremy Lin (second from left) and his brother, father, and grandmother

LOVE OF THE GAME

Jeremy's parents, Gie-Ming and Shirley, were born in Taiwan. Gie-Ming says his love of basketball was one of the reasons they came to the United States.

Lin went to Palo Alto High School. He was an excellent student. He was also a star guard on his school's basketball team. He led Palo Alto to a 31–2 record as a junior. The next year Palo Alto went 32–1 and won the state championship. Lin was named to California's all-state team.

Lin was one of few star Asian-American players. He had to deal with **prejudice** and a lack of respect.

prejudice—an opinion about others that is unfair or not based on facts

Lin celebrates with his Palo Alto teammates after winning the Division II state basketball championship in 2006.

"I do get tired of it; I just want to play. But I've also come to accept it and embrace it. If I help other kids, then it's worth it." – Jeremy Lin

Lin hoped to get a college **scholarship** to play basketball. But no top basketball schools offered him one. He chose to attend Harvard University. Harvard is one of the nation's best schools. But the university doesn't offer athletic scholarships.

"I wasn't the biggest or most explosive [high school player]. But I was disappointed and thought I had been overlooked." — Jeremy Lin

scholarship—money provided for a student's education

Lin struggled on the court during his first year in college. He was playing against stronger and faster athletes. But he worked hard and got stronger. He became a great passer and scorer. As a junior, he scored 27 points in a big win over Boston College. He was named to the All-Ivy League first team as a junior and a senior.

Lin became one of the greatest Harvard basketball players ever. He ranks fifth on the school's all-time scoring list and second in steals. He also ranks fifth in **assists**.

assist—a pass that leads to a score by a teammate

CHAPTER 3

NBA SENSATION

Lin hoped a team would pick him in the 2010 NBA **Draft**. Eight teams invited him to work out before the draft. But none of them picked him.

Lin later signed with the Golden State Warriors. But he didn't play much as a rookie. The Warriors **waived** him before the 2011–12 season. The Houston Rockets signed and waived him too. Finally, he joined the Knicks.

draft—the process of choosing a person to join a sports team
waive—to release a player

Lin with his parents,
Shirley and Gie-Ming,
after being signed by the
Golden State Warriors

Lin hardly played at first. He got his chance February 4, 2012, when two Knicks stars couldn't play. He exploded for 25 points. He instantly became a starter. The Knicks won seven games in a row. Lin made a game-winning free throw in the final seconds against the Minnesota Timberwolves. He also hit his big 3-pointer against the Raptors.

No one had ever seen an NBA star rise so quickly. Fans loved it. They called Lin's sudden stardom Linsanity.

HOT START

Lin scored 136 points in his first five NBA starts. That's the most by a player since the NBA and the American Basketball Association merged in 1976.

CHAPTER 4

LINSANITY

Lin's story is rare. It usually takes years for an NBA player to rise to fame. But Lin was an underdog who became an overnight sensation. He was all over news shows and on magazine covers. People loved his humble attitude.

Lin's 2011–12 season ended early after he injured his knee. Some fans wondered whether Lin could continue his success. Others pointed to his quickness and good decision-making skills. They believed he would be a solid point guard in the NBA for years to come.

TIMELINE

1988—Lin is born August 23 in Los Angeles, California.

2005—Lin leads Palo Alto High School to a 31–2 record and is named his league's MVP.

2006—Lin leads Palo Alto High School to a 32–1 record and the state championship; he is again named league MVP; he begins college at Harvard.

2008—Lin is named to the All-Ivy League second team.

2009—Lin's 27 points help Harvard defeat 17th-ranked Boston College on January 7; he is named an All Ivy League first teamer.

2010—Lin graduates from Harvard and signs with the Golden State Warriors.

2011—The Warriors and Houston Rockets waive Lin; he later signs with the New York Knicks.

2012—Lin becomes New York's starting point guard February 6; he scores 136 points in his first five starts.

GLOSSARY

assist (uh-SIST)—a pass that leads to a score by a teammate

draft (DRAFT)—the process of choosing a person to join a sports team

prejudice (PREJ-uh-diss)—an opinion about others that is unfair or not based on facts

rookie (RUK-ee)—a first-year player

scholarship (SKOL-ur-ship)—money provided for a student's education

waive (WAVE)—to release a player

READ MORE

Doeden, Matt. *Greatest Sports Stars.* Sports Illustrated Kids. Mankato, Minn.: Capstone Press, 2011.

Knobel, Andy. *New York Knicks.* Inside the NBA. Edina, Minn.: ABDO Pub., 2012.

Smallwood, John. *Megastars 2011.* New York: Scholastic, 2011.

INTERNET SITES

FactHound offers a safe, fun way to find Internet sites related to this book. All of the sites on FactHound have been researched by our staff.

Here's all you do:

Visit *www.facthound.com*

Type in this code: 9781620656266

 Super-cool stuff! Check out projects, games and lots more at www.capstonekids.com

INDEX